great spaces
home interiors

Edition 2006

Author: Jacobo Krauel
Publisher: Carles Broto
Editorial Coordinator: Jacobo Krauel
Graphic designer & production: Pilar Chueca
Text: contributed by the architects,
edited by Núria Rodríguez and Marta Rojals

© Carles Broto i Comerma
Jonqueres, 10, 1-5
08003 Barcelona, Spain
Tel.: +34 93 301 21 99
 Fax: +34-93-301 00 21
E-mail: info@linksbooks.net
www. linksbooks.net

great spaces
home interiors

INTRODUCTION

Interior design is one of the fields of architecture that has most evolved in recent decades. The new tendencies and lines of evolution are clearly shown in the use of materials, the forms of construction and styles.

In response to demanding clients with a wide range of stipulations, architects working in interior design have been forced to explore new fields, to open up new paths that are adapted to the taste of new generations. The challenge often consists of interpreting and giving a creative value to the demand and needs of the client, who is at times excessively preoccupied by purely commercial needs or by the contaminations of fleeting fashions. This is why in all interior design one can see an effort to reach the perfect synthesis between function and aesthetics, between the essential and the non-essential.

In this book you will find solutions of the most diverse types, but there are perhaps a few lines of action that could be considered common to the new generations of interior design: a certain tendency to clear the spaces of decorative objects that conceal the lines of the architecture, the almost systematic elimination of the habitual resources used to disguise the load-bearing structures, an obvious tendency to transparent spaces with few spatial divisions, and the recurring use of light and colour as an integral part of the architectural solutions.

In summary, this book presents a selection of the most interesting proposals in interior design, showing a return to more humanised concept based on the profound relationship of man with his inhabited space.

Carlo Donati

Loft A

Photographs: Matteo Piazza

Milan, Italy

Loft A is located in a typical banister house in the centre of Milan. It is the result of the unification of three different units. Actually the loft was subdivided in two small flats, one on the ground floor one on the first floor, linked by a long passage to a recently built block, a wide art gallery. The connection of these three units which differed in their characteristics, was to produce a major architectural challenge.

The first projectual step consisted of defining the connection between the three separate units.

The old, long and blind passage at the entrance was transformed into a double egg-shaped volume, two pure bodies inserted one into the other following axis with different directions.

The helicoidal stairs lead from the first oval to the bedrooms of the upper floor.

The access to the main bedroom is in the second oval, this area is completely independent, with a wide bathroom, wardrobe, and direct access to the private inner garden.

The rooms on the ground floor weave in and out of each like characters in a story. Entering the kitchen it is possible to understand the arrangement of the living area, whose spaces rotate around the interior garden, which is the pivot of the whole apartment.

The living room is an open space where the dining, home theatre, fireplace and conversation area are in sequence. The route is completed by a small swimming pool, on which the mezzanine-study faces (related to a relaxation area, a sauna, a shower and a bathroom) scenographically projected like part of the living, just separated by huge fixed glasses from the rest of the space.

The architectural choices were supported by innovative materials and avant-garde technical solutions. Corian was used for the furniture, while the woods are refined and unusual essences, the floors are all made of resins.

The technical solutions involved the use of carbon fibres with structural functions, the heating system was realized with ground radiant panels of the last productive generation. They have the double functions of heating during wintertime, and of refreshing and de-humidifying during summertime.

The lighting plant is innovative and guarantees maximum flexibility in lighting and the automation of all home - equipment via remote control, personal computer or mobile phone.

The old, long and blind passage at the entrance was transformed into a double egg-shaped volume, two pure bodies inserted one into the other following axis with different directions.

Lower floor plan

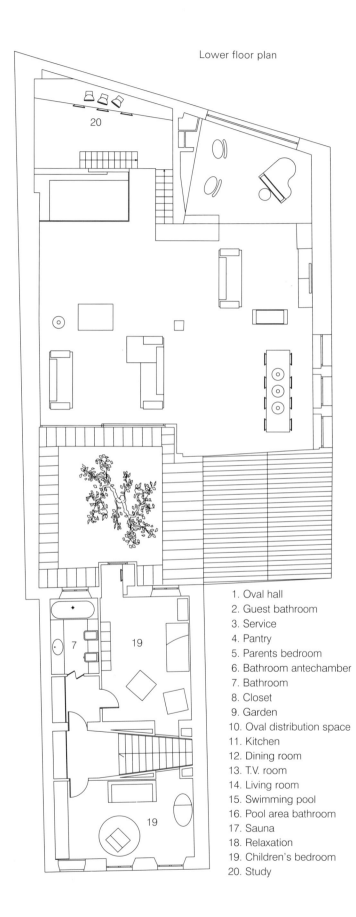

Upper floor plan

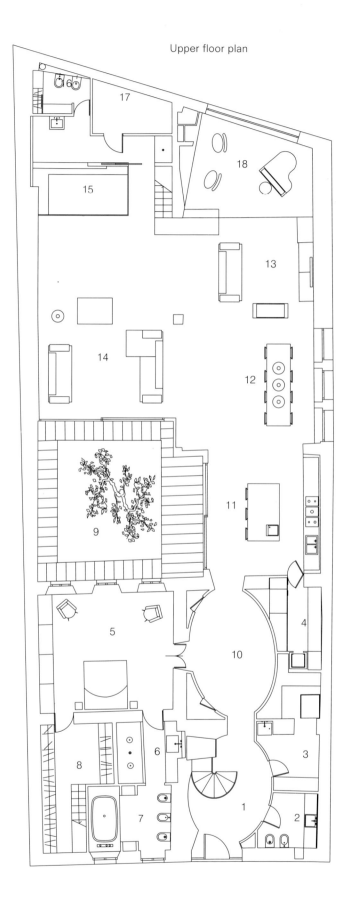

1. Oval hall
2. Guest bathroom
3. Service
4. Pantry
5. Parents bedroom
6. Bathroom antechamber
7. Bathroom
8. Closet
9. Garden
10. Oval distribution space
11. Kitchen
12. Dining room
13. T.V. room
14. Living room
15. Swimming pool
16. Pool area bathroom
17. Sauna
18. Relaxation
19. Children's bedroom
20. Study

The lighting plant is innovative and guarantees maximum flexibility in lighting and the automation of all home - equipment via remote control, personal computer or mobile phone.

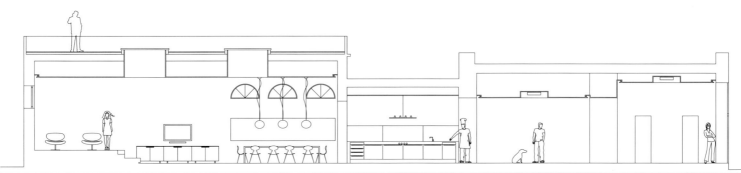

Relax - Kitchen - Entrance Section

Garden - Kitchen Section

Bathroom - Parent's bedroom - Garden - Living - Swimming pool Section

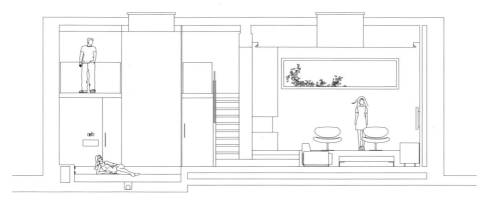

Swimming pool - Living Section

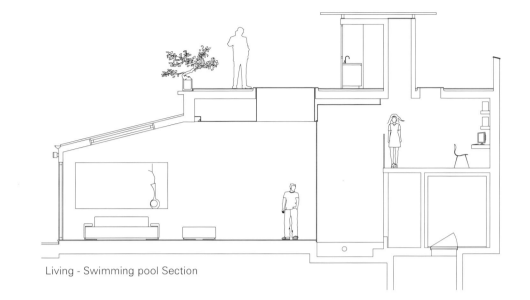

Living - Swimming pool Section

Drewes + Strenge architekten bda

Rheda Penthouse

Photographs: Christian Richters

Rheda - Wiedenbrück, Germany

The two-floor bachelor's penthouse is the result of joining together two previously separate apartments. The open loft atmosphere was achieved by eliminating most of the walls and partitions. In order to maintain the radiant floor heating which was already there, the ceiling was left untouched. Both verticality and a sensation spaciousness were gained by opening up the staircase, and making of it a stark visual focus and a bold design element.

The main floor consists of a central living space with kitchen, dining and relaxation areas. The attic above is the master bedroom suite which includes a secluded private study.

The bathroom is connected to the bed by means of a large window which exposes the bathtub and the sink. The shower and the toilet are discretely hidden in a chamber clad in black Bisazza glass mosaic.

The materials used throughout the penthouse are limited to the following: black MDF, Nero Assoluto granite, cold rolled steel, concrete and epoxy.

This project included the complete design of all the furniture and lighting, relulting in a seamless unification of two nondescript spaces.

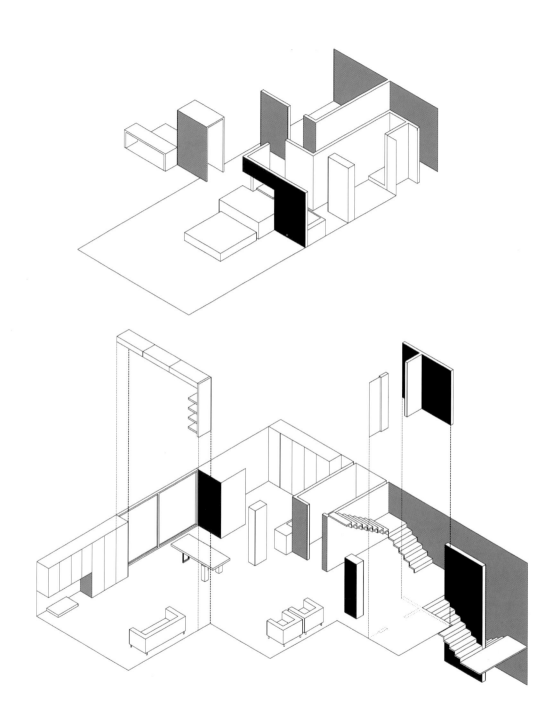

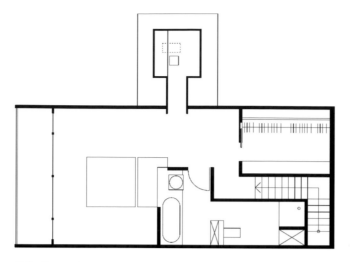

Attic floor plan

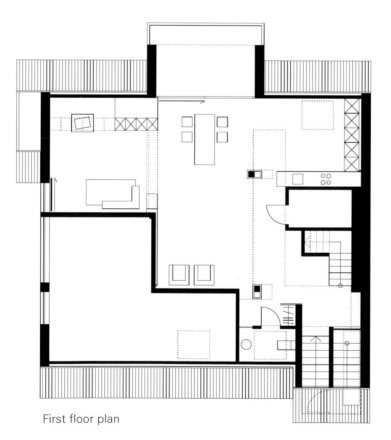

First floor plan

The bathroom is connected to the bed by means of a large window which exposes the bathtub and the sink. The shower and the toilet are discretely hidden in a chamber clad in black Bisazza glass mosaic.

Kei'ichi Irie + Power Unit Studio

Y House

Photographs: Hiroyuki Hirai

Chita, Aichi, Japan

Suburban sceneries are sad. Modernization, industrialization, and IT innovation have ripped down the cities' inner landscapes, destroying to shreds what had been left of nature in the suburbs. Cities in the pre-modern times used to devise way of reconciling and co-existing with nature that they had destroyed in the course of their own construction. But the suburbs have abandoned it, swayed by stereotyped urban models. To this day, excessive faith in industrial development and forces of technology is conducting hideous violence across the country. Such historical bruises would continue to prevail among suburbs throughout Japan as long as there are those who believe that urban recovery may be improved by means of industry, science and technology. Dignity and serenity of landscape are now on the way of extinction.

Y house is found among a row of houses up on a hillside. A landscape with retaining walls in conflicting wilderness as a result of development-its imperviousness is just menacing. It is in no way possible to impose a full-scale change on such devastation. But we may build a house that is neither destructive nor violent.

Like a Musical Instrument

We decided to avoid tinkering with the inclination as much as possible and create a space isolated from the surrounding painful landscape. Once inside the building, the floor slopes down along the topography leading to a large cantilever floor, directly open the forest. The only major opening in this house, it frames the forest scenery through the big sliding doors with black rims. The opening facing the street serves only to introduce light through the translucent glass, except for one black-rimmed window which frames a small view of the town.

Walls on both sides of the cantilevered space are slightly slanted outward to avoid assimilating themselves into the surrounding retaining walls. These slanted surfaces intersect, preliminary to being named floors or walls, and resonate with each other to create a soundless acoustic space. The plates of the body (as in a violin) producing such echoes is the thin surface of concrete, only 15 cm thick. The realization of uniformity of thickness (15cm) among all surfaces allowed the architecture to take on such musical property. Motions such as the slow sway of forest trees, birds' flight, or traces of rain feed the space with a variety of speeds. They reverberate between slanted surfaces and reach the ear.

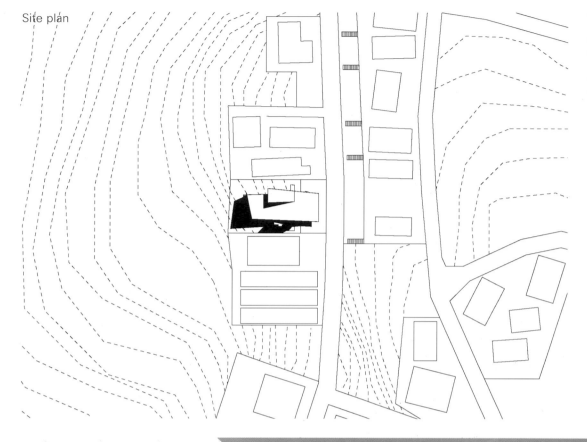

Y house is found among a row of houses up on a hillside. The architects may build a house that is neither destructive nor violent.

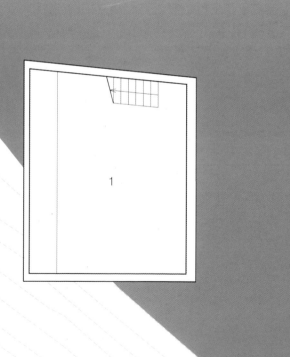

Floor -2 plan
1. Bedroom

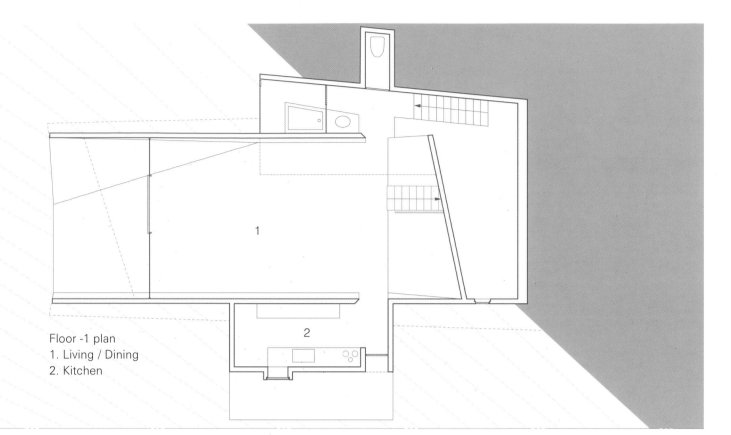

Floor -1 plan
1. Living / Dining
2. Kitchen

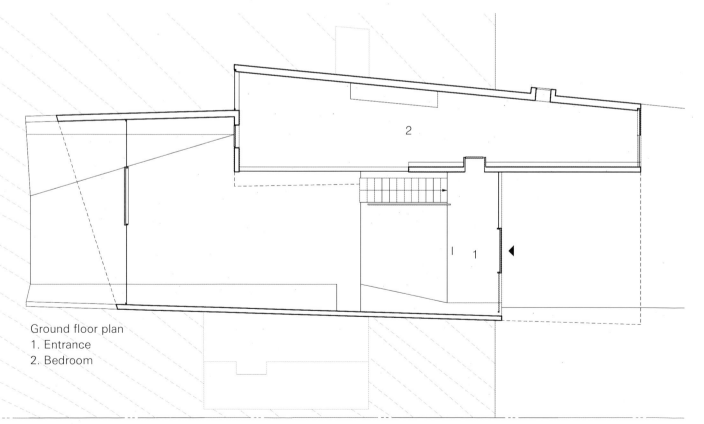

Ground floor plan
1. Entrance
2. Bedroom

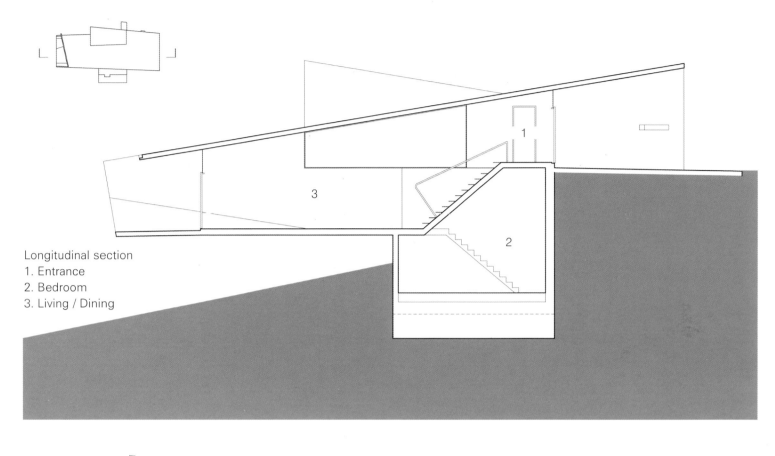

Longitudinal section
1. Entrance
2. Bedroom
3. Living / Dining

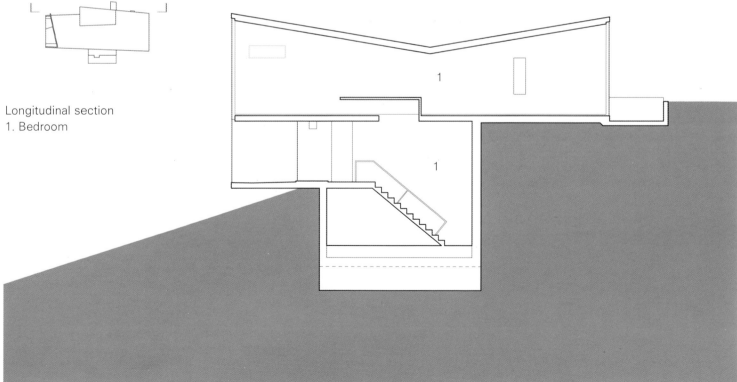

Longitudinal section
1. Bedroom

37

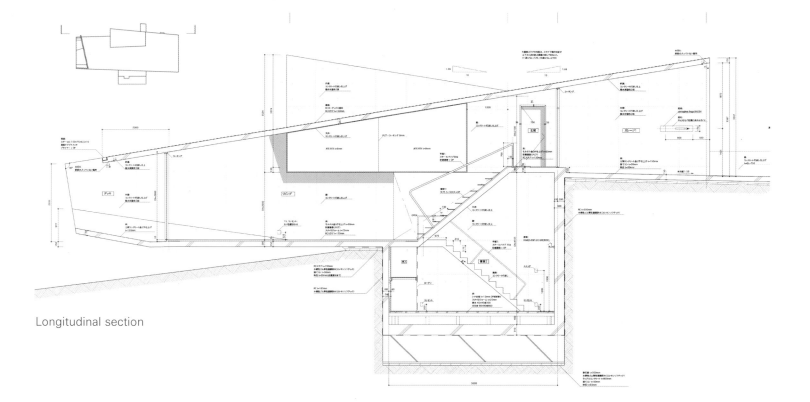

Longitudinal section

Johnson Chou

Yolles Residence

Photographs: Volker Seding

Toronto, Canada

When Eric Yolles (son of renowned Canadian structural engineer Morden Yolles) wrote a program detailing every aspect of his new loft to be considered, he concluded with two words: "think penitentiary". The intention was not to create a space that would be harsh and cold, but one of calm and repose. He wanted a contemplative space with a minimum of spatial distraction, one with particular attention to materials and detail - that his loft would not contain any overt decorative embellishments or gratuitous design flourishes.

Housed in a converted warehouse in downtown Toronto, the 2,000SF loft is organized in a conventional strip with industrial windows at one end. All non-structural walls were removed and a wall dividing the public and private areas was replaced with a 30' sandblasted glass screen. Layering with sliding partitions, views through rooms change as these panels move and entice with sections of clear glass - transforming and revealing one area as they conceal another. The largest of these partitions - a dramatic section of 16' stainless steel - separates the bedroom from the living room. Inspired by the "Panopticon", a prison type that allows the warden to view all inmates from a single position, the design amplifies the voyeuristic pleasures of surveillance: a 10-inch strip of clear glass through which one can view the living areas from the sunken slate bathtub - true bachelor-pad indulgence, complete with built-in candleholders.

Experimenting with the act of viewing, the bathing area is like a stage set where one enacts the self-conscious performance of both watching and being watched.

Designing everything essential to living directly into the space is an integral part of the designer's creative philosophy; creating 'a narrative of habitation' - or building a 'script' for the client. The bed (aluminum-clad and king-sized) is cantilevered from the wall so it appears to hover in mid-air. A glowing bedside 'command module' constructed of sandblasted glass slides open to access light switches, thermostat and telephone. Aluminum floor to ceiling storage closets span the entire length of the bedroom, holding and hiding all of the client's belongings.

Though bare and elemental, the liberal use of glass, aluminum, stainless steel and concrete impart a particular glow and warmth to the interior, specific to the materials themselves. Subtle nuances and reflections in the slate and metal reveal themselves through lighting, playing off surfaces, lending a sculptural, ephemeral quality to the bed and freestanding vanity. Using light as a theatrical element, halogen and fluorescent fixtures are used in a variety of combinations to re-define space, use, and mood. Intersecting ceiling-mounted recessed fluorescent lighting provides ambient lighting while halogen and accent lighting are strategically positioned to subtly highlight existing and new architectural details and textures.

1. Foyer
2. Powder room
3. Guest bedroom
4. Kitchen
5. Living room
6. Laundry
7. Bedroom
8. Storage
9. Vanity
10. Bath
11. Toilet
12. Shower

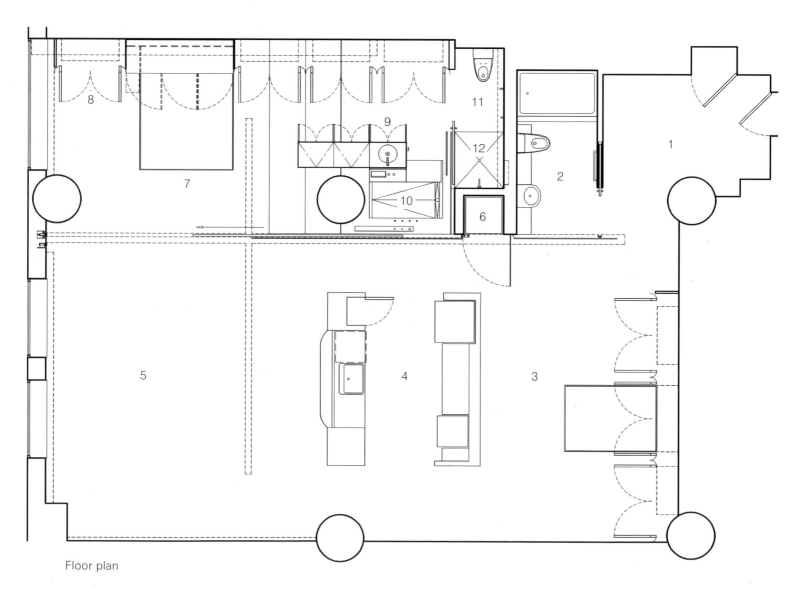

Floor plan

Though bare and elemental, the liberal use of glass, aluminum, stainless steel and concrete impart a particular glow and warmth to the interior, specific to the materials themselves.

Bonetti Kozerski Studio

DK Apartment

Photographs: Matteo Piazza

New York, USA

The project features a master bedroom suite that includes a dressing room and bathroom gallery; a large living room and dining room that is connected to the terraces with a stone platform that runs throughout; a meditation room and "spa" bathroom, a chef's kitchen and preparation kitchen/pantry, a house manager's office and a maid's suite. The house is furnished with custom furniture designed by Bonetti/Kozerski Studio, Asian antique pieces and some contemporary pieces. Floors in the public spaces feature cross cut travertine in 1.2 meter square tiles, while the bathrooms use larger pieces of travertine on the walls and floors. Flooring in the master suite is a tatami style wool sisal, in a color matching the stone. The walls are highly polished Venetian stucco in an ivory color. The ceilings are custom colored ivory paint. The kitchen features a combination of natural teak, stainless steel lower cabinets, frosted glass upper cabinets and a basalt volcanic stone counter top.

The project involved the combining of two large apartments at the top of a 1929 building on Central Park West. Even before starting the design we concentrated our efforts on finding a way to have the client's full understanding of the spatial concept in order to win her trust in something that was going to be quite different from the traditional New York upscale apartment. We built a full-scale model of the design after demolishing all the non-structural walls of the apartment. We employed a theatrical company that built fabric walls held in place by springpoles. Reading a plan or fully understanding a model can be complicated for a client: building a full scale model permitted the client to literally walk into the design, comprehend it and familiarize himself with it before committing to the expense. The fabric walls could be instantly moved, giving the opportunity to verify a spatial solution, change it or incorporate the client's suggestions. Once satisfied with the layout and the furniture, which was also mocked up full size, we did a survey and transferred the final design on paper. Some of the architectural solutions derived directly from techniques employed in the full size model. The lighting was designed by Arnold Chan from London's Isometrix, who collaborated with us before on the Donna Karan Store on Madison Avenue.

1. Entrance
2. Gallery
3. Yoga room
4. Bathroom
5. Dining room
6. Media room
7. Living room
8. Kitchen
9. Butler's pantry
10. Service area
11. Private gallery
12. Dressing room
13. Master bedroom
14. Terrace

Floors in the public spaces feature cross cut travertine in 1.2 meter square tiles, while the walls are highly polished Venetian stucco in an ivory color.

Roberto Silvestri

A house in Piazza Navona

Photographs: Ernesta Caviola

Rome, Italy

Designing the interior spaces of a house allows you to work with emotions, to shape rooms that will hold inside feelings, angers, passions, moods. "The house is the life coffer," Le Corbusier used to say. Upon this concept we have based the project for the house of an italian film director; a house that had to gather the private world and the public life of the owner. A house that had to be, at the same time, "coffer" and "theatre" of life.

During the designing process, we have spent a long time together with the client talking about cinema, art, cooking, books, and being careful not to touch on technical problems. The idea was to create an interior space shaped exactly around the client's character and desires, without thinking too much about functional problems that, in this way, would have been naturally solved. For this reason, deep knowledge of the client has been so important; his ideas, his way of moving, his passions and tastes have been the functional program.

Working with these purposes, we managed to make a very sensitive place, a rich but not overwhelming space, a strong but warm and cozy place at the same time. We believe that it is impossible for mankind to live in geometrically perfect spaces, to stay in architecturally pure forms. For this reason, we have designed a rigorous house that speaks with feelings and the imperfections of human life. So the space is extremely open and fluent. The rooms are strictly connected, but at the same time, each single traditional room is still visible in the structure of the house. The house is not loft space, but is a real house divided into rooms that suit the contemporary way of Italian living.

The access to the house comes from above, walking on a three-step stair made of Travertino Navona slabs put on a light iron structure. The living room has very little furniture. The main character of the room is the front wall: dark, brown, velvety, non-homogeneous. This is the first of the two walls that are covered in Cort-ten: rusted iron usually used in exteriors. This material is absolutely perfect for our purposes: it is warm, strong and capable of giving a beautiful atmosphere to the whole room. The two rusted walls form the space of the studio: a small, intimate and high tech place that can easily be transformed into another sleeping room.

The outside terrace is connected to the kitchen that is completely open to the rest of the house. In front of the kitchen, two openings in the ancient wall show the history of the place with its historical bricks made of Roman Tufo. This creates a strange contrast with the modern materials of the new project such as the aluminium wainscoting which is included within the wall itself.

The private spaces are very small: a bedroom and a bathroom. The first one has been designed around the client, so it is a very small place with just a bed and a wardrobe, both made of natural wood. Very different from this is the bathroom; a place for private luxury completely different from the rest of the house. The floor is made of big slabs of red marble that strongly contrast with the white of the walls that are partially covered with a very particular kind of tiles: the same tiles that the client saw in the Paris underground while he was starting an unforgettable love story.

Floor plan

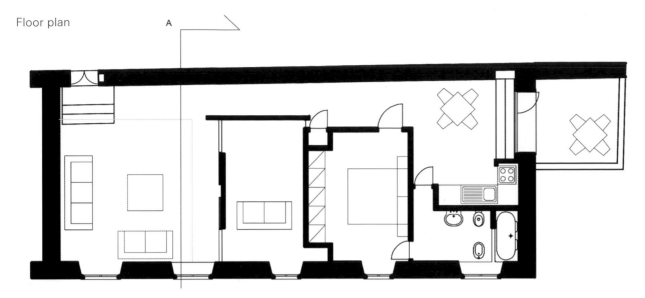

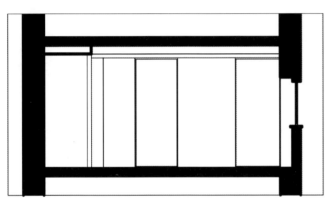

Cross section

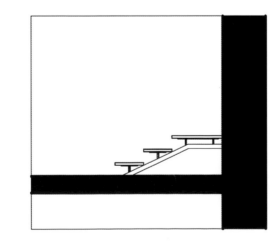

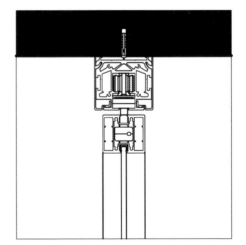

Detail A of door

Detail B of door

M. J. Neal

Ramp House

Photographs: Barcelona Films

Austin, Texas, USA

The house sits on an in-fill lot close to downtown, in a neighborhood dominated by 1930s and 40s bungalows. In accordance with zoning constraints, the building is pushed to the back of the lot, allowing the south side to be planted with a large entry garden. A vine-covered trellis acts both as a fence and a brise soleil, filtering the light and providing a sheltered approach to the house along a gravel path defined by garden foliage.

On the inside, the play on the senses continues through the lpe ramp that provides vertical circulation through the house. One of the architect's aims was to slow down the pace of life, and this inspired a multilevel floor plan that uses the sun's movements to create playful effects with natural light. Beams of light from the east are filtered through colored glass squares and create changing patterns and hues in the different rooms.

The entrance leads to an impressive foyer and a steel and lpe wood ramp that runs along the center of the interior and defines the space. Bookshelves are nestled between the two runs of the ramp and accessible from both sides creating, and an oversized landing provides space for reading or study.

On the lower level, concrete floors lead to the two bedrooms, which have access to the garden and courtyard. A conversation pit, which can double as a spare room, is at the back of the house.

The upper floor consists of flexible living, dining and entertaining space, making the most of the limited space. The kitchen includes black granite counters, extensive cabinets and rubber floors made from recycled tires. A custom-designed spiral staircase near the living area leads to a rooftop deck with panoramic views over downtown Austin.

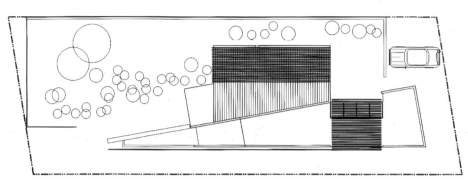

Site plan

The main structural component is structural insulated panels (SIPS), which provide the envelope and roof. The wedge shape that encloses the ramp is clad in red anodized aluminum panels, and the rest of the exterior is finished in Aquatec, a plywood with a natural preservative that protects the wood while allowing it to change over time.

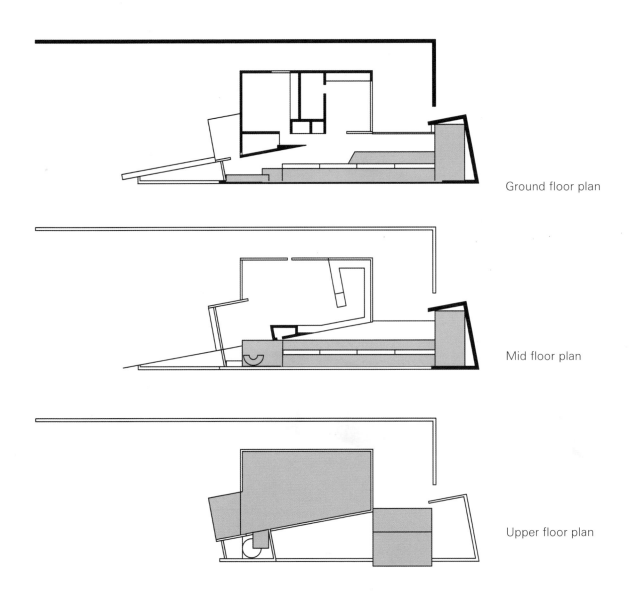

Ground floor plan

Mid floor plan

Upper floor plan

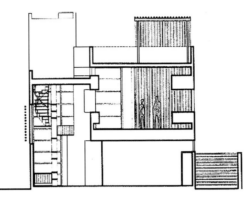

Cross section

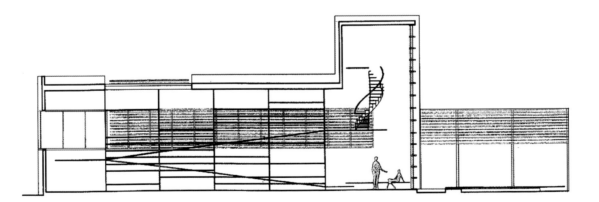

Longitudinal section

Eulàlia Sardà

Apartment Sant Vicenç

Photographs: José Luis Hausmann

Sant Vicenç de Castellet, Spain

The apartment is on two floors. On the lower floor are the living room and dining room as a single space, and the kitchen which is independent, separated by a partition and a swing-door. The main area displays a strikingly generous space that reaches 5m at the highest end, as the ceiling has a 30% gradient. On the other hand, the kitchen has been designed to contain the maximum amount of storage space, so as to leave the dining room as free as possible from clutter. The dining room furniture was all designed by Eulàlia Sardà and made to order. Halogen lamps are used throughout the house, but in the kitchen there are also energy-saver built-in downlights.

One of this project's undeniable requirements was to ensure that all the areas have adequate access to natural light, which the careful distribution plan has achieved satisfactorily.

From the dining room there is an open stairway leading upstairs. The steps are of solid beech wood supported by a metal structure, with a railing of stainless steel cable.

The kitchen furniture and cabinetry are of natural cherry wood, combined with frosted glass and aluminum frames, stainless steel handles, 3 cm thick 'Blanco Cardenal' white granite worktops and adjacent vertical surfaces. The remaining kitchen walls have been finished in white Venetian stucco. All the kitchen equipment is of stainless steel.

All the outdoor aluminum items are galvanized matt aluminum grey. Indoor carpentry is of steamed beech wood and all the flooring is of beech except in the kitchen and the bathrooms, where Italian stoneware tiles with an imitation-stone finish define the wet areas.

The kitchen furniture and cabinetry are of natural cherry wood, combined with frosted glass and aluminum frames.

SAMARK Arkitektur & Design AB

Turning Torso Apartment

Photographs: James Silverman

Malmö, Sweden

The building itself was designed as a sculptural landmark, thus calling for an ambitious interior that would live up to its remarkable exterior. The very shape of the building presented as many difficulties as it did unique opportunities. For example, the number of doors leading from the staircase core / elevator shaft as well as the thickness of the concrete core brought with them certain prerequisites and obstacles.

On the other hand, the plan enabled four excellent "living room positions" per floor - rooms spanning corners or spaces placed along the fully glazed façade. The shape of the plan also naturally inspired rather large apartments in relation to the number of rooms, since connecting partitions facing the leaning façade had to be avoided.

The aim was to create large living rooms that would be directly linked to partly open kitchens. The entryways are also open, generously proportioned spaces, whose floors are clad in pol-ished Swedish limestone, a material also used on all of the window sills along the facades.

In most of the large apartments the bedrooms have been separated from the more "public" areas, which are constituted by the entrance hall, living room, dining area and kitchen. Oiled oak is the flooring used in all other areas, except the bathrooms.

Massive full-height doors in light glazed oak and sliding doors close off the bedrooms and bathrooms in an otherwise very open floor plan. Accentuated architrave and trim complements the doors at floor height. All wardrobes have been completely built into the walls.

The bathrooms have been fully tiled in a small clinker on the floors and a somewhat larger tile on the walls. The countertops in the bathrooms and kitchens are available in three varieties of granite and one of the walls in the kitchen is clad in ceramic tiling. The cupboards, which come in a range of materials to choose from, such as light glazed oak, white glossy laminate or aluminum with oak trimmings, have been custom designed for the project.

The ceilings throughout are smooth and white and the ceiling height in the living room is raised to slightly more than 2700 mm. The kitchens, bathrooms, toilets and laundry rooms are supplied with recessed spotlights.

Offices floor plan

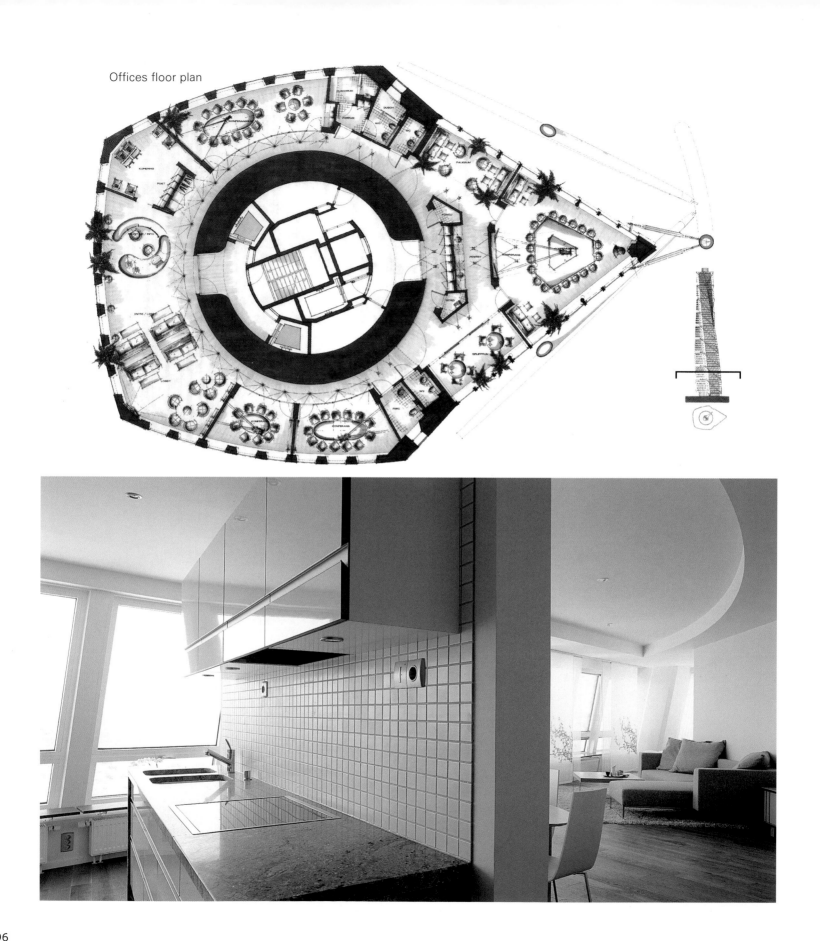

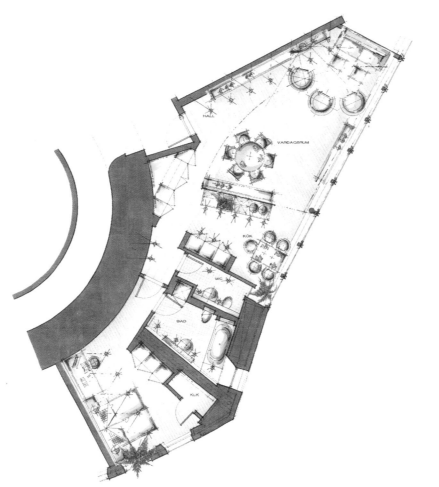

Apartment 242

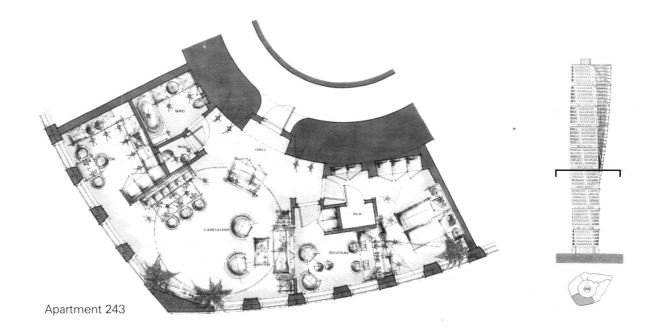

Apartment 243

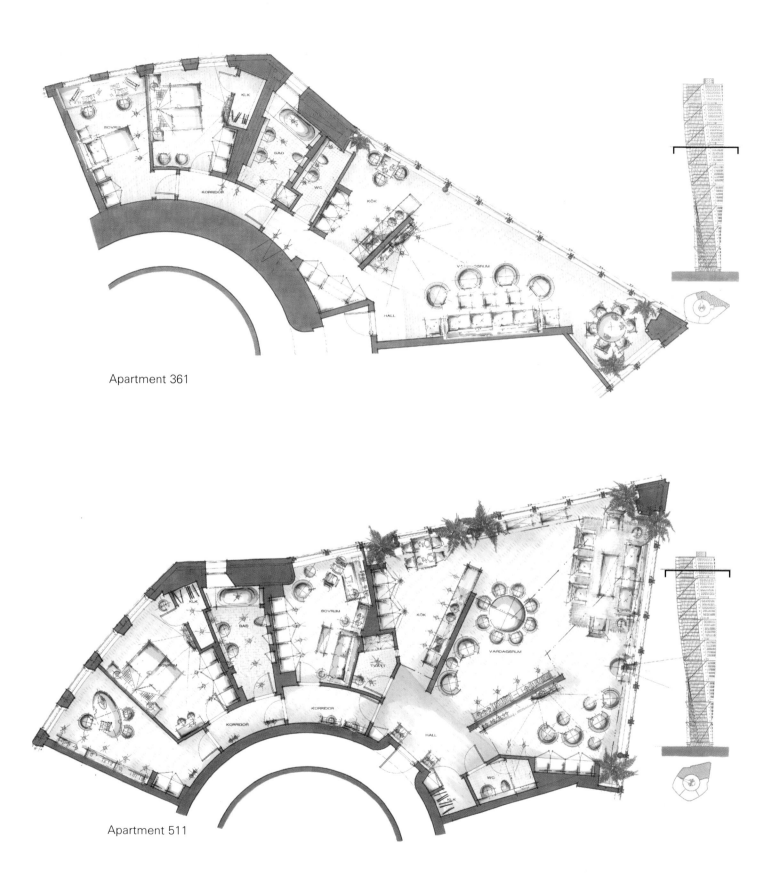

Apartment 361

Apartment 511

98

Gracia Studio

House GA

Photographs: Pablo Mason, Eduardo de Regules

Tijuana B.C, Mexico

The characteristics of the site influenced the concept of the house, which was based around resolving two main two issues. The first was the desire for a house with views, in a residential area that only had the potential for distant panoramas. This led the architects to divide the house into two intersecting elements, so that the two parts of the house look in towards each other - a modern house looking at a modern house. This idea, which dictated the design concept, created a kind of oasis of modern architecture surrounded by the tiled roofs that are common in the surrounding area.

The second main issue was related to making the best of a limited budget. The native soil on the site was found to be at 24 feet above street level, and the engineer recommended building pylons to ensure a solid construction. Instead, the architects decided to remove the unusable soil and raise the house by 10 feet. This meant gaining a 4,000 square foot basement/patio on a 4,875 square foot lot, and a 5,250 square foot house, with the same budget that building pylons would have implied.

The resulting building is based on two elements, one clad in wood and the other in white polycarbonate, with galvanized metal detailing. The interior is dominated by simple lines and large spaces, with the variable ceiling heights that are made possible by the two intersecting shapes. Enclosed spaces and views to the interior courtyards and across to the other half of the building give the whole house a modern feel, creating a self-referential space, independent from its surroundings.

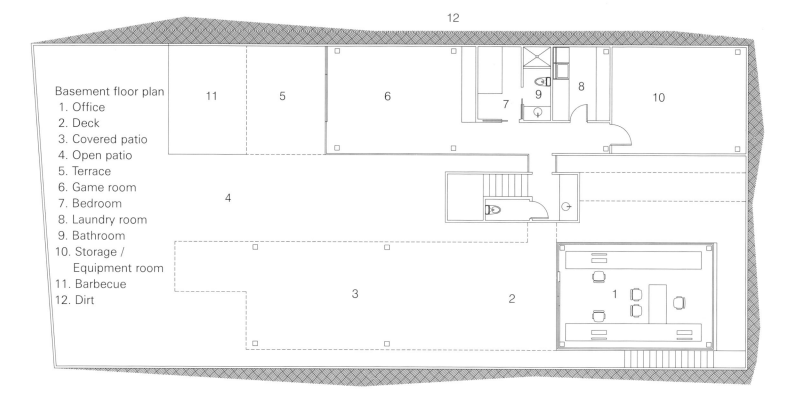

Basement floor plan
1. Office
2. Deck
3. Covered patio
4. Open patio
5. Terrace
6. Game room
7. Bedroom
8. Laundry room
9. Bathroom
10. Storage /
 Equipment room
11. Barbecue
12. Dirt

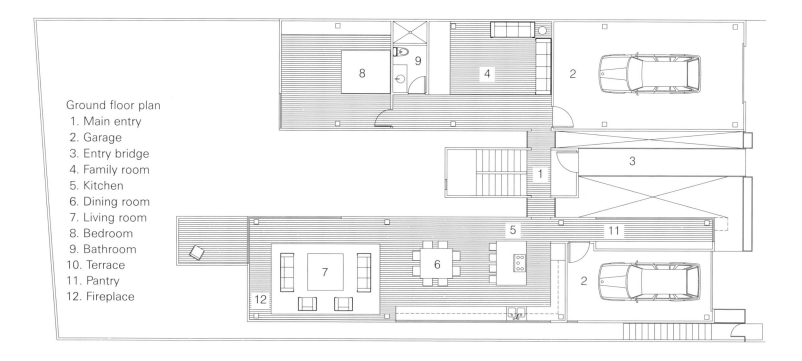

Ground floor plan
1. Main entry
2. Garage
3. Entry bridge
4. Family room
5. Kitchen
6. Dining room
7. Living room
8. Bedroom
9. Bathroom
10. Terrace
11. Pantry
12. Fireplace

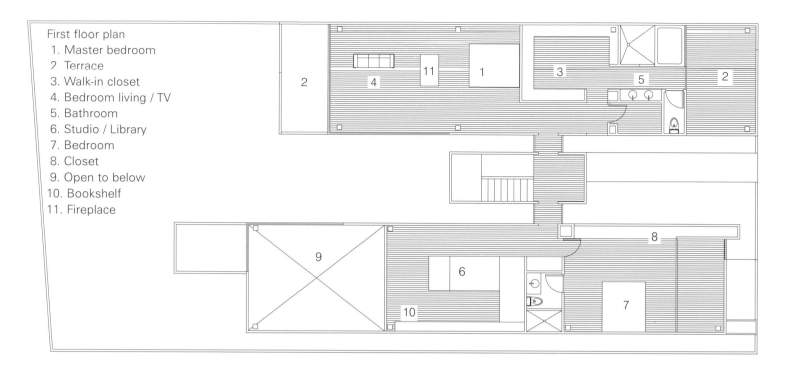

First floor plan
1. Master bedroom
2. Terrace
3. Walk-in closet
4. Bedroom living / TV
5. Bathroom
6. Studio / Library
7. Bedroom
8. Closet
9. Open to below
10. Bookshelf
11. Fireplace

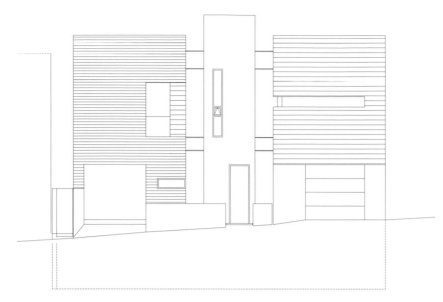

East elevation

West elevation

North elevation

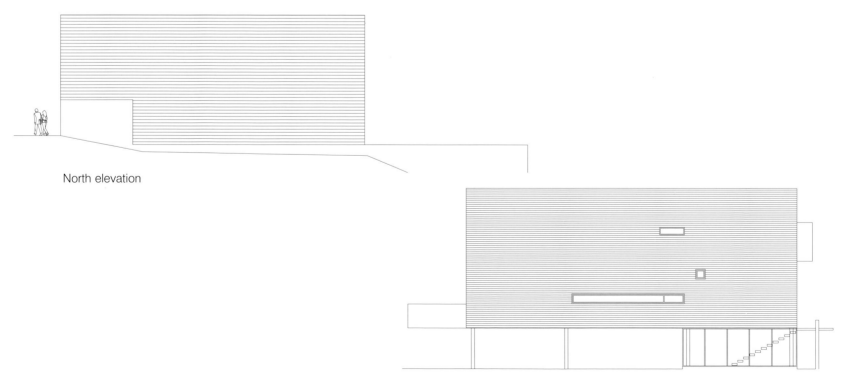

South elevation

115

Glen Irani

Hover House

Photographs: Undine Pröhl

Venice, California, USA

The Hover House is a live/work prototype designed to resolve typical problems experienced in the contemporary home-office by putting a greater emphasis on the quality of the professional environment. The house envelops 3,500 square feet on three levels, including a studio for the architect, an artist studio for his wife, a residence with guest quarters and outdoor living space, within the confines of a 30 x 90 foot lot along the canals of Venice, California.

The project responds architecturally to the problems facing professionals who work at home through three main strategies. Firstly, by providing opportunities to rest the mind and body during long working hours through amenities such as the garden, terraces and swimming pool. Secondly, it encourages engagement with the community by placing the working area on "prime real estate" - the ground level - with high transparency and accessibility to the public space. Thirdly, it addresses the need for workspace accessibility and privacy by isolating the workspaces from the living areas. The architecture studio is the only habitable space in the garden, so it also readily converts to a living area by sliding the desks to one end on integrated rails.

The massive house that hovers above the ground level program is focused around a large, C-shaped "sun-court" oriented towards the southwest. On the second floor, a children's playroom and the community areas all open onto the sun-court through large sliding glass panels. All the furniture on this level is lightweight and exterior rated so that the courtyard can be furnished quickly and flexibly - as a playground, living area, art studio, dance floor, sunning deck, etc. Children's play areas are all visible from "adult" areas.

The artist's involvement in developing spaces, building systems like windows and objects within them like cabinetry, expresses his interest in manufacturing buildings as opposed to constructing them. Reflecting the preference for manufacturing practices, other than the foundation, framing and wall finishes, much of the house is actually factory fabricated.

Over 40 colors throughout the house, most visible from every area in the house, arose from a fledgling color theory devised by the architect and artist. This theory, while being peripherally concerned with color hue relationships, focuses primarily on the light-reflectance relationships between colors and the vibration of light that occurs when many colors unite in one space. These vibrations articulate movement, mass, time and materiality.

The floor-to-ceiling glass windows flood the interior spaces with light and provide visibility that unifies the house. The colors, the landscaped garden and the swimming pool are part of the strategy to improve the quality of professional and family life by allowing the mind and body to be inspired and rejuvenated.

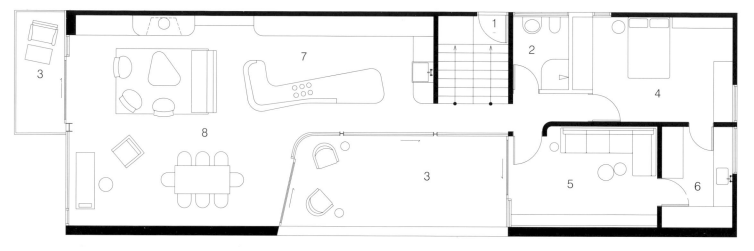

Ground floor plan

1. Entry
2. Bathroom
3. Outdoor terrace
4. Bedroom
5. Den / Guest bedroom
6. Laundry
7. Kitchen
8. Living / Dining room
9. Master bedroom
10. Master bathroom
11. Painting studio

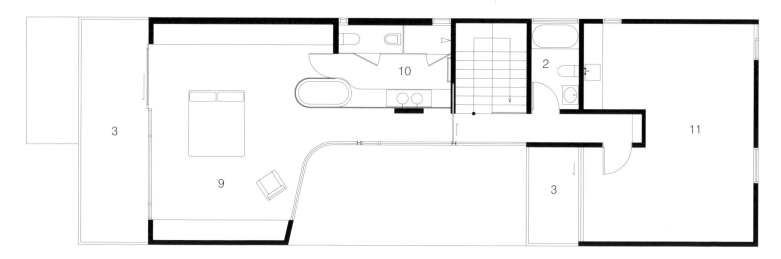

First floor plan

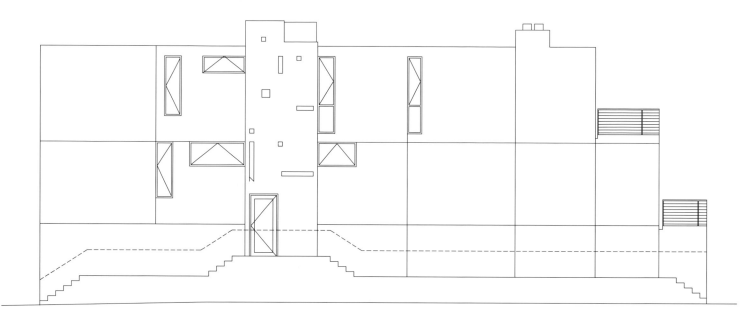

Elevation

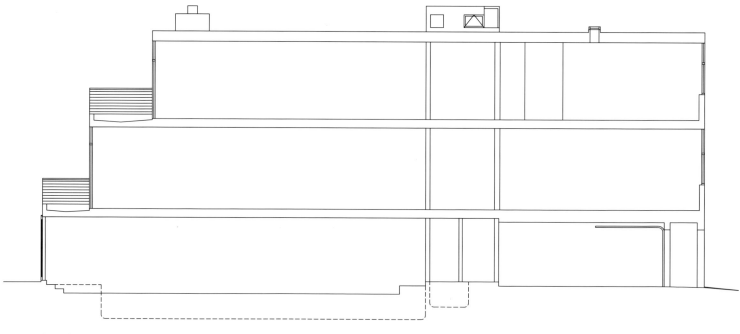

Longitudinal section

Elevation

Elevation

1. Studio / Office
2. Lap pool
3. Spa
4. Entry

5. Outdoor terrace
6. Hallway
7. Kitchen
8. Master bedroom

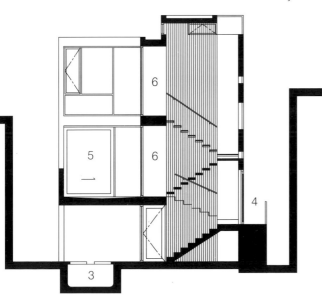

Cross section

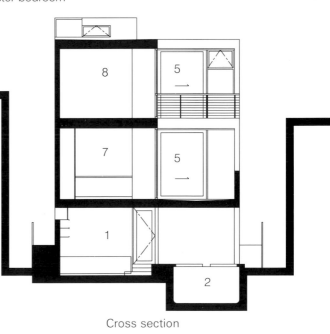

Cross section

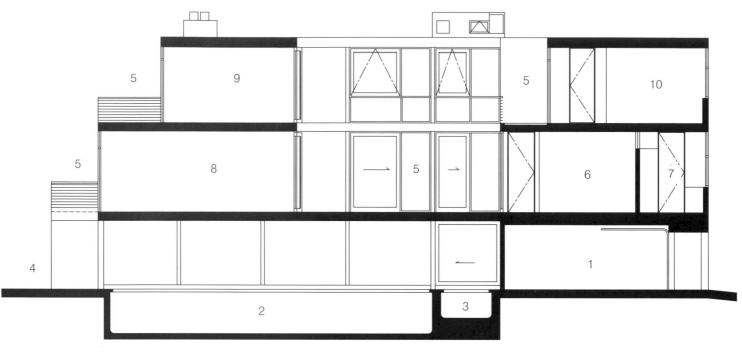

Longitudinal section

1. Garage / Workshop	4. Garden	8. Living / Dining room
2. Lap pool	5. Outdoor terrace	9. Master bedroom
3. Spa	6. Den / Guest bedroom	10. Painting studio
	7. Laundry room	

Takao Shiotsuka

Atu House

Photographs: Kaori Ichikawa

Ohnojo-city, Fukuoka Prefecture, Japan

The site is on the boundary where the residential area meets the forest. The tiered landscape and a small waterway are the main geographical features, and it is surrounded by trees. A little sunlight penetrates through the foliage, creating the appealing feeling of a dense forest. The architects decided to bring the external environment into the interior of the house through the design and the choice of construction materials.

In three directions, the building is used as a large glass window, with the color of the surrounding trees projected onto its surface. The weather outside and the passing of time changes the expression of the house at each moment. A glass window reaches from the floor to a height of about 1.8 meters, and minimizes the need for artificial light. The glazed patterned glass abstracts the scenery to a green-hued mosaic. In order to bring the surrounding green deep into the interior of the rooms, the indoor furniture and other materials are white.

The architects and the client preferred to secure a bigger space rather than highly finished materials. The high-ceilinged space effectively enhances the surroundings in the shape of a tiered stand for dolls, with a height difference indoors. A middle floor is used to project the ventilation and colors of the trees indoors.

The circular light from the ceiling changes according to the different sized spaces, giving the appearance of a random effect and mirroring the environment that is constantly changing. The outer wall is a wave-like steel plate, which reflects the color of the sky and the trees.

"ATU" is the name of the daughter of the house. Her physical disability, which means she can't go into the outdoors by herself, inspired the concept of the house. The idea, which was successfully realized, was to project the surrounding scenery inside and envelop the space and the family in the green forest.

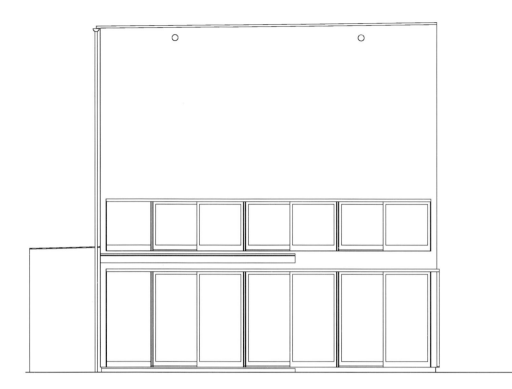

West elevation

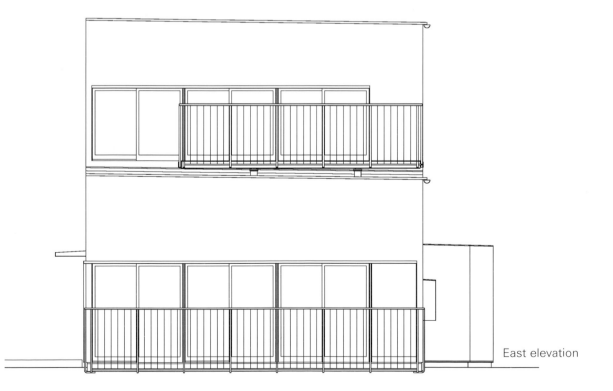

East elevation

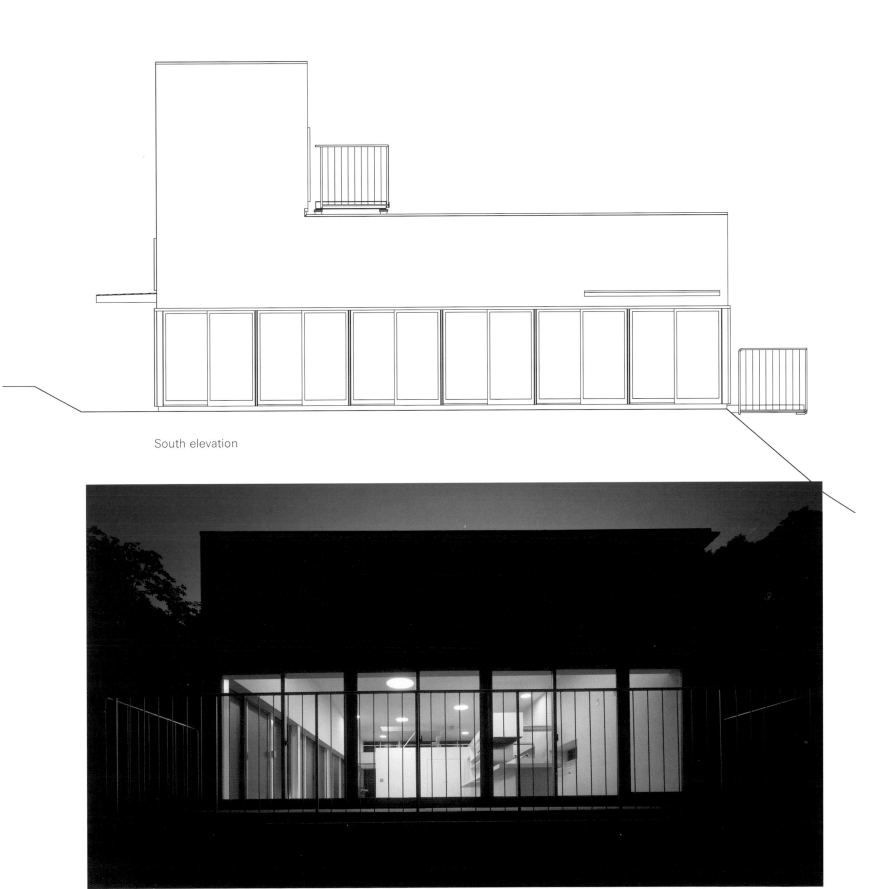

South elevation

137

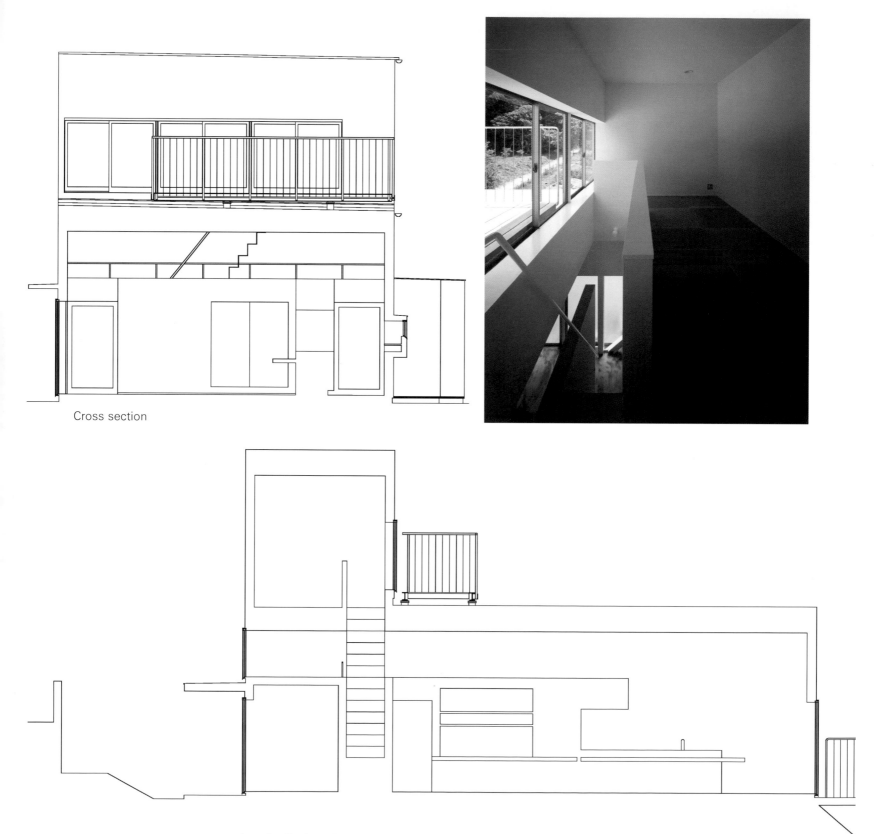

Cross section

Longitudinal section

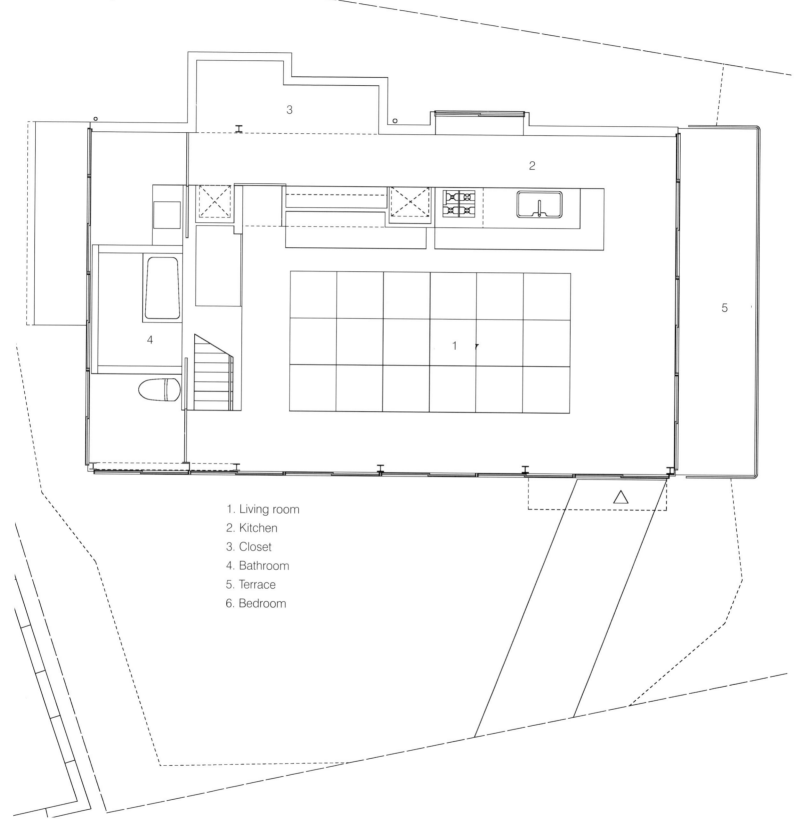

1. Living room
2. Kitchen
3. Closet
4. Bathroom
5. Terrace
6. Bedroom

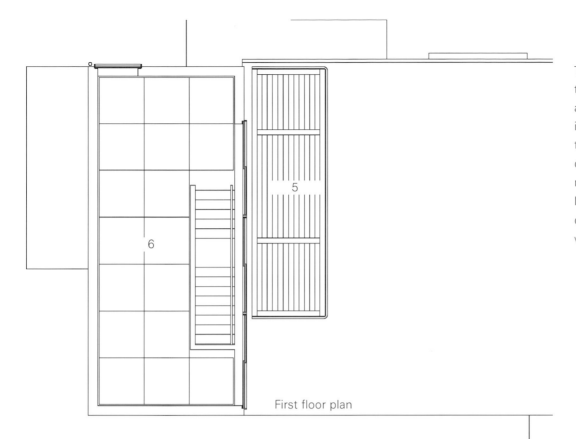

The design and construction materials draw the spacious feeling and natural colors of the surrounding landscape into the interior of the house. The large glazed windows that dominate the house minimize the need for artificial light and create a constantly changing patterns based on the weather conditions outside.

First floor plan

Marpillero Pollak Architects

Duane Street Live Work Loft

Photographs: Jeff Goldberg/Esto

New York City, USA

128 -132 Duane Street was built in the 1860s as a manufacturing facility comprised of three twenty-five foot-wide bays. Two bays were demolished with the widening of Church Street in the 1920s to facilitate open-pit construction of the Eighth Avenue IND Subway (A, C, E).

Conversion of the ground floor and basement spaces began with the removal of a 12' wide segment of the rear yard extension, and a corresponding 12' x 18' segment of the first floor. The two cuts transformed the dark basement into a light-filled atrium, its 26' high window opening up to an enlarged garden. The garden is a constructed ground which supports vegetation and light-reflecting white riverstone; angled mirrors, set on an adjacent building reflect strips of sky and clouds, layering this view with the abstracted landscape of the garden.

Continuous full-height exposure of the west brick wall of the loft and construction of the ceiling as a unified element enable light to penetrate deep into the spaces. Original timber joists are displaced to wrap and frame the intervention, introducing a delay in its perception.

Work and living spaces are both organized on three levels: basement, ground floor, and mezzanine, with the office at the front facing the street. A hybrid construction of vertical circulation and book storage mediates between work and living spaces: the office stair-bookshelf extends from basement to mezzanine, shifting from solid below to transparent above; the house stair wraps around two sides of the 20' high bookcase, as it shifts from public to private living areas.

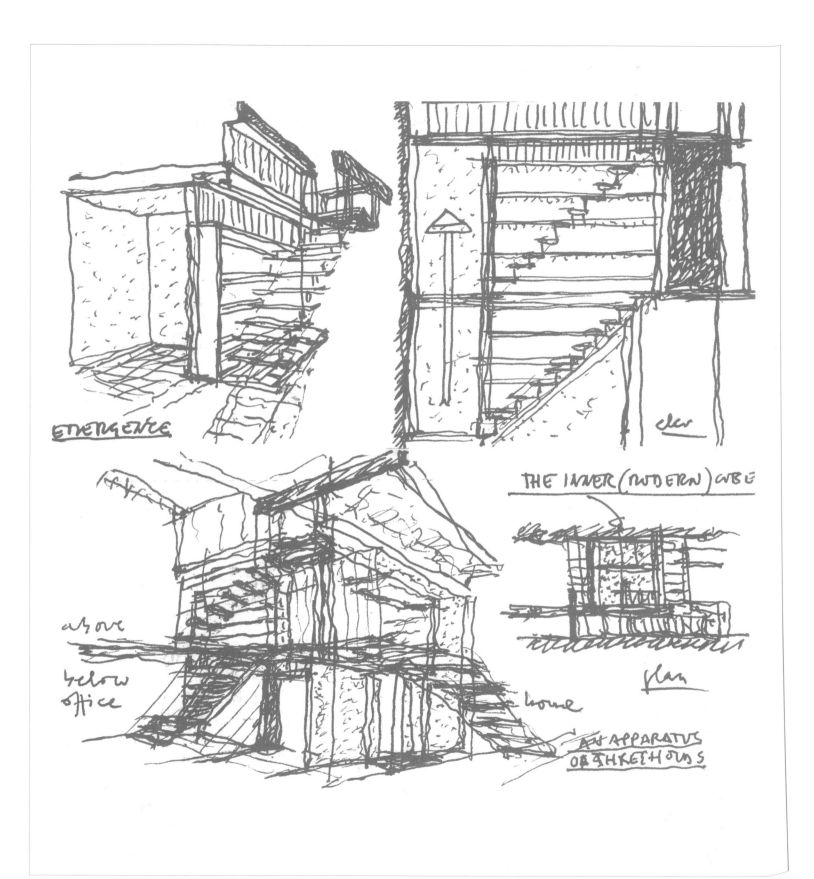

EMERGENCE

THE INNER (MODERN) CUBE

elev

above

below
office

home

plan

AN APPARATUS
OF THRESHOLDS

Continuous full-height exposure of the west brick wall of the loft and construction of the ceiling as a unified element enable light to penetrate deep into the spaces.

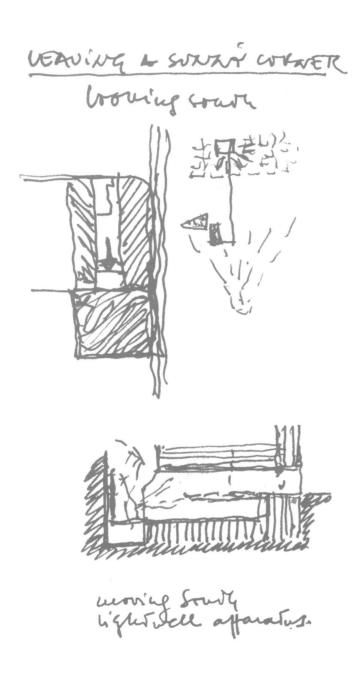

LEAVING A SUNNY CORNER

looking south

moving south
lightwell apparatus.

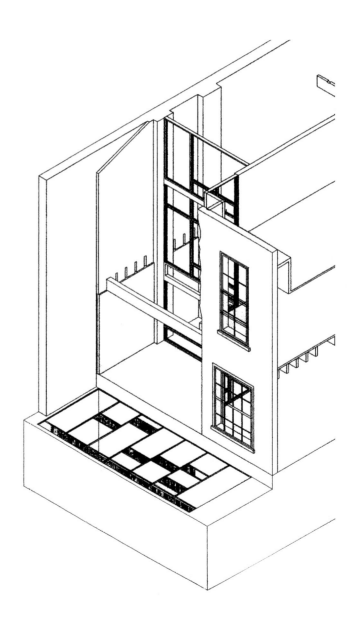

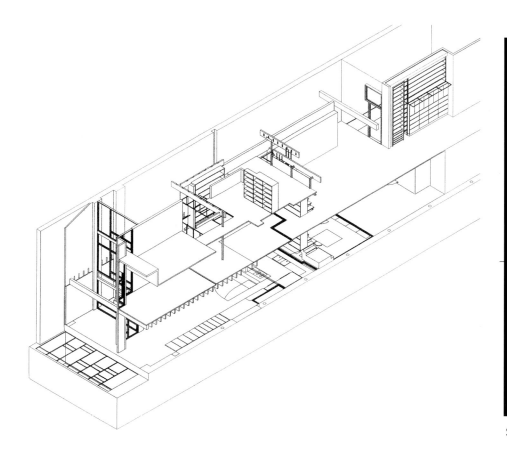

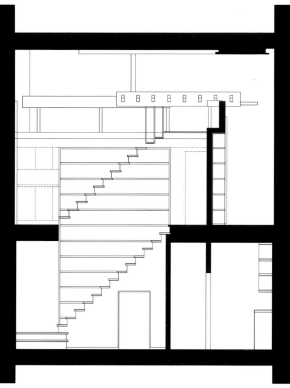

Section CC thru office bookshelf stair

Conceptual collage learning from "Mesa Verde"

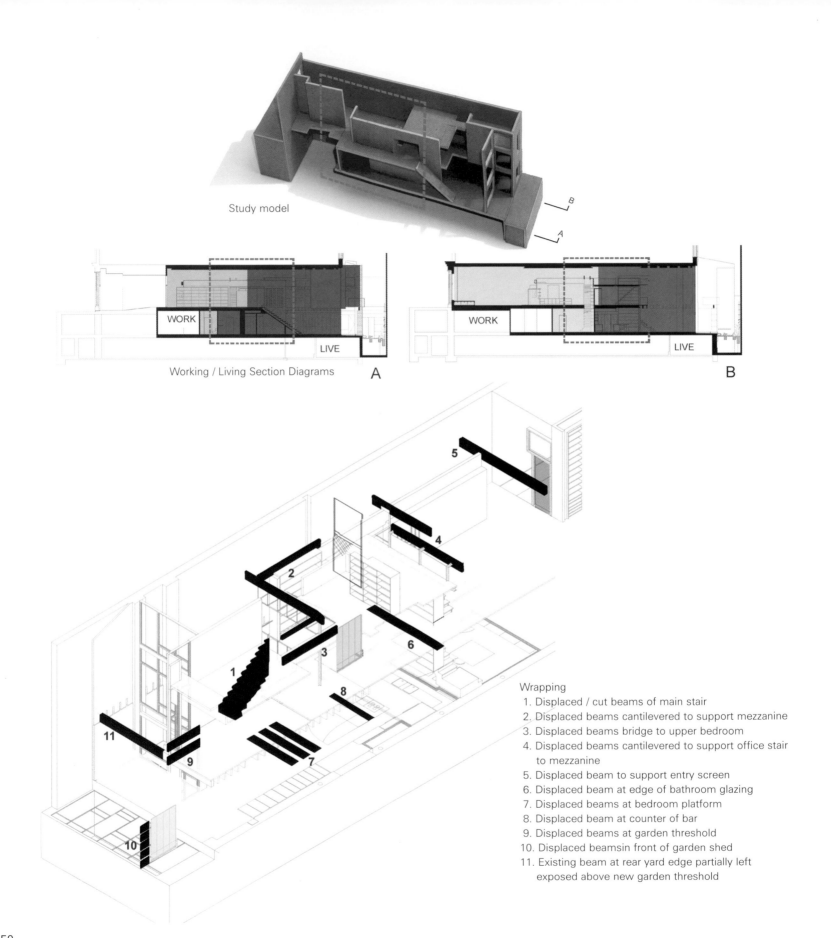

Study model

Working / Living Section Diagrams

WORK

LIVE

A

WORK

LIVE

B

Wrapping

1. Displaced / cut beams of main stair
2. Displaced beams cantilevered to support mezzanine
3. Displaced beams bridge to upper bedroom
4. Displaced beams cantilevered to support office stair to mezzanine
5. Displaced beam to support entry screen
6. Displaced beam at edge of bathroom glazing
7. Displaced beams at bedroom platform
8. Displaced beam at counter of bar
9. Displaced beams at garden threshold
10. Displaced beamsin front of garden shed
11. Existing beam at rear yard edge partially left exposed above new garden threshold

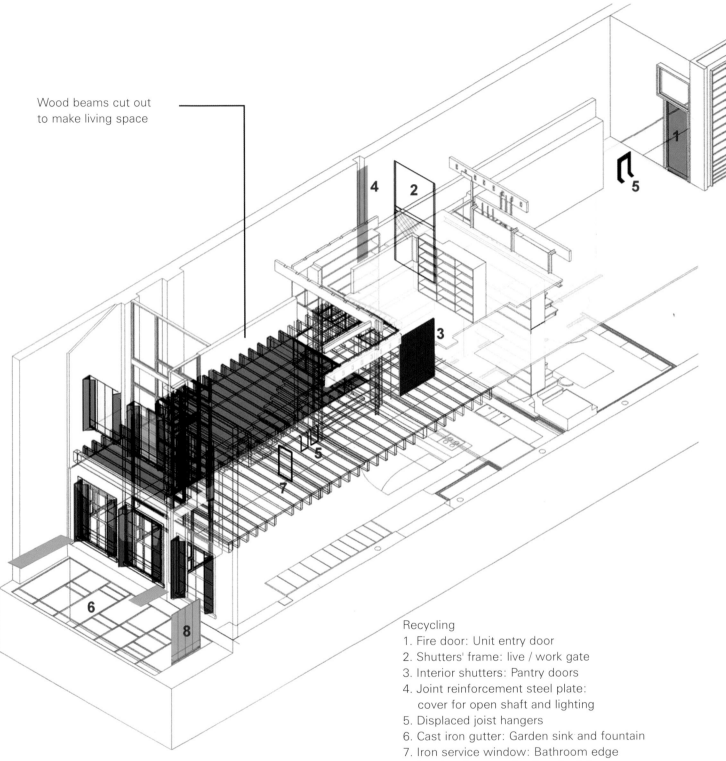

Wood beams cut out
to make living space

Recycling
1. Fire door: Unit entry door
2. Shutters' frame: live / work gate
3. Interior shutters: Pantry doors
4. Joint reinforcement steel plate:
   cover for open shaft and lighting
5. Displaced joist hangers
6. Cast iron gutter: Garden sink and fountain
7. Iron service window: Bathroom edge
8. Interior shutters: Garden shed doors

Subtracting

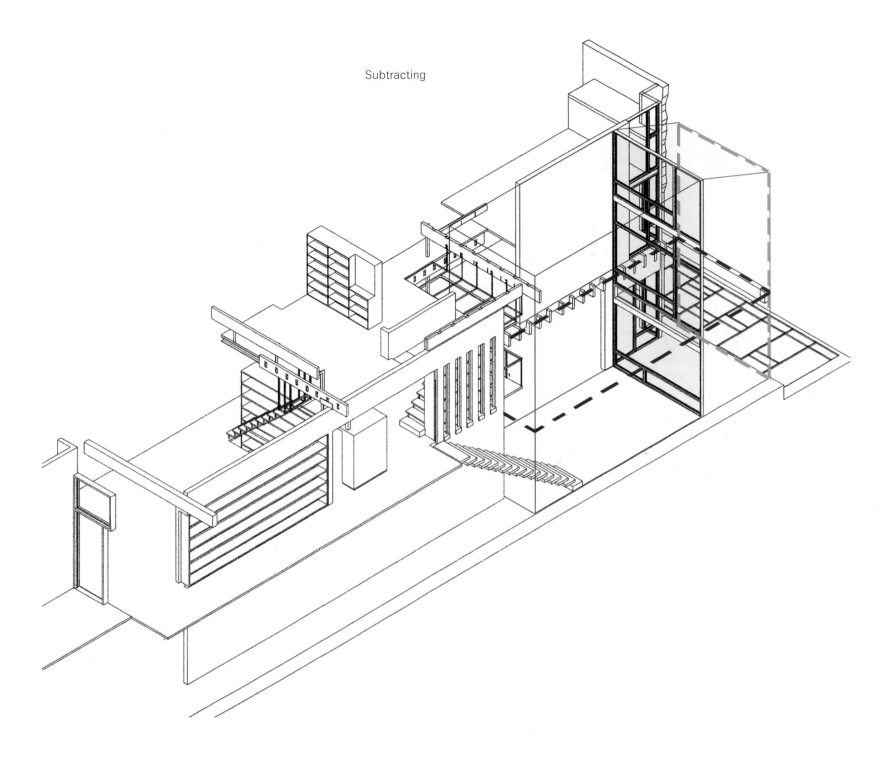

Portion of first floor subtracted to make living space ━ ━ ━ ━ ━ ━ ━

Portion of rear yard extension subtracted to make garden ━ ━ ━ ━ ━ ━ ━

153

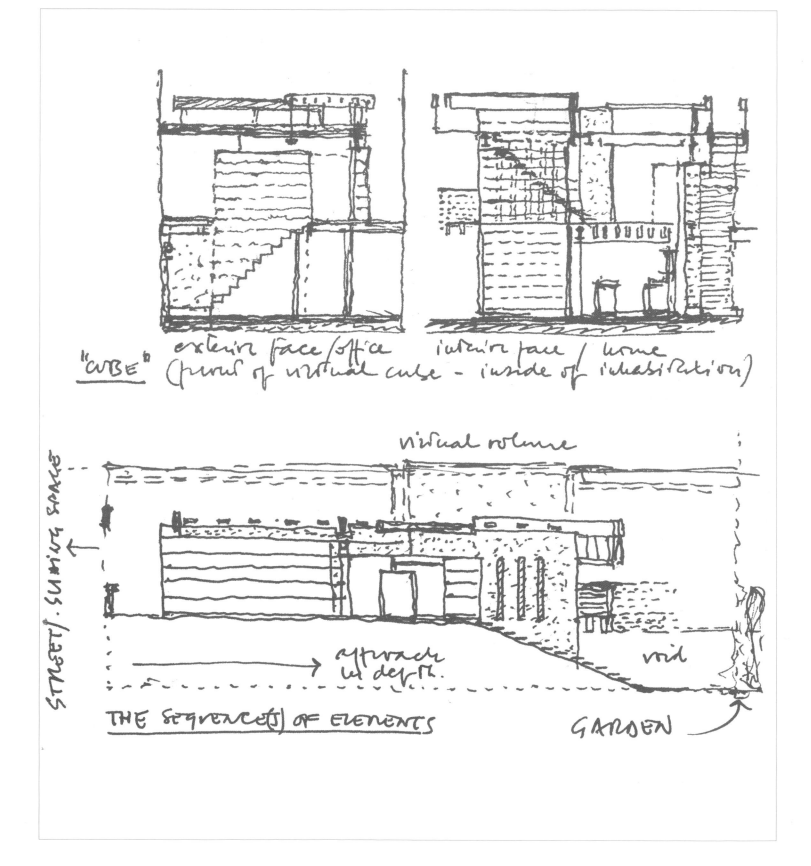

"CUBE" exterior face / office   interior face / home
(front of virtual cube — inside of inhabitation)

virtual volume

STREET / . SLIDING SPACE

approach in depth.

void

THE SEQUENCE(S) OF ELEMENTS

GARDEN

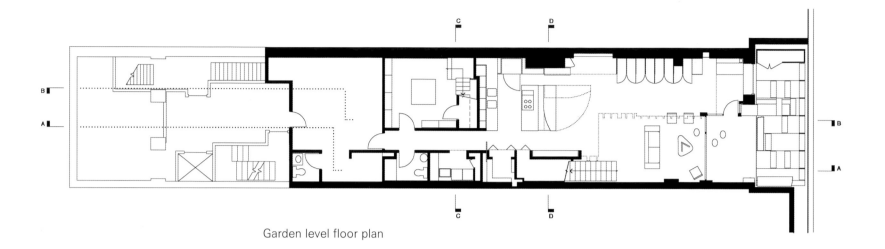

Garden level floor plan

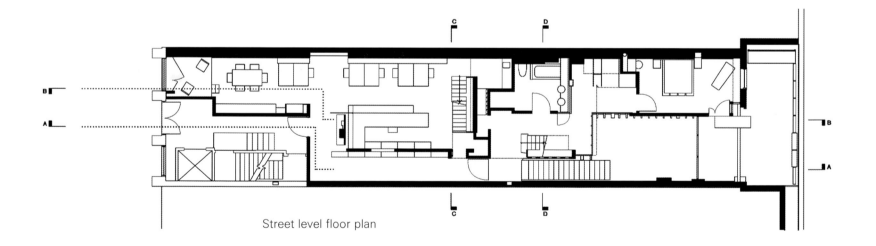

Street level floor plan

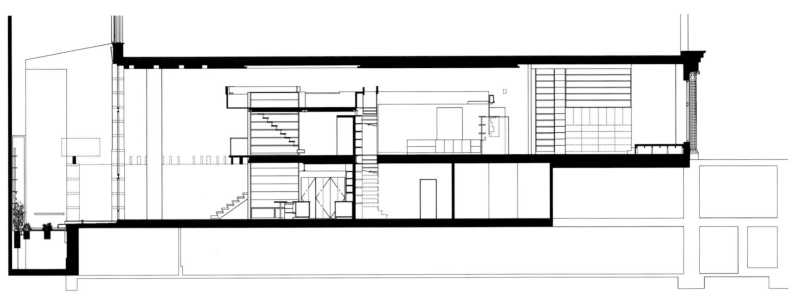

Section BB looking West

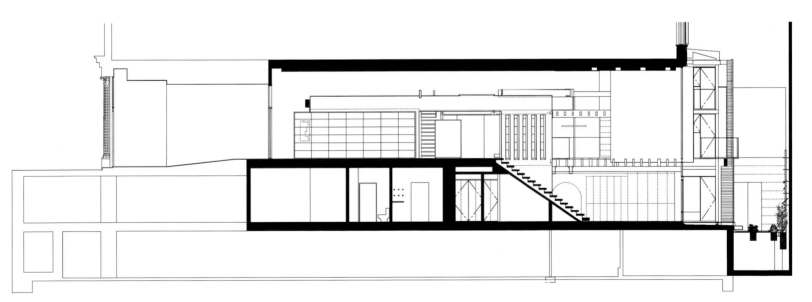

Section AA looking East

Jordi Galí

Apartment in Barcelona

Photographs: Jordi Miralles

Barcelona, Spain

At the start of this project, the top slab of the pre-reform apartment was higher than it is now, the walls and flooring were greatly deteriorated and there were no dividing walls.

The program called for a single-occupant apartment, for which a diaphanous and unified space was created, installing dividing walls only in the bathroom.

Due to their visually degraded state, all of the perimetral walls were clad in Pladur up to the height of the beams of the slab, leaving a small portion of the top of the original walls bare. The five-centimeter space left between the Pladur and the original wall was put to use with the installation of indirect perimetral lighting throughout the apartment, thereby heightening the drama of the old wood beams and vaults. The entire kitchen volume, including the cupboards and shelves, were also done in Pladur. The cupboards were kept at a low height, the top part of the walls being clad in a Pladur partition which conceals the smoke extractor and a fireproof panel which, when lowered, hides the kitchen range and work area.

The paving was finished in cement dyed a greenish-gray. The sink is held up on the sides by transparent glass panels, visually tying it to the bedroom.

The bright light entering the interior of the dwelling is filtered by a venetian blind system.

Simone Micheli

Bussotti Residence

Photographs: Mario Corsini

Venturina, Livorno, Italy

The Bussotti House is a work of global architectural, an expressive space in which furniture and surfaces only partly reveal their given primary function, transcending their traditional role to relate in original new ways. The visitor discovers a pseudo-museum-like space, an installation of the architecturally unexpected, in which furniture becomes an art that is both surprising and moving.

The main feature of the spectacular entrance space is the wide hall, with a floor of oak planks, out of which the elegant kitchen area emerges: this consists of a sculpture and an island, both painted white, with a stainless steel range, illuminated from above by white ceramic floodlights. The non-kitchen conceals the accessories and avoids its stereotyped role as container. The cupboards are equipped with push-open mechanisms. On the entrance wall, a large liquid crystal TV screen violates the ethereal grace of the creased white textile wall covering.

The oak stairway rises sculpturally; the railing describes a spiral that starts close to the ground but reaches a height of six feet when it gets to the top; its thickness also varies on the way up. The first floor parapet is a sheet of Visarm tempered glass, illuminated by a line of spotlights in the floor.

From the first floor landing you see the main room, featuring an oak floor and a pillar and beam painted bright green.

The materials are used with care and the few incisive signs are manifested in the furniture, with pure and essential lines: a hidden cupboard is virtually second white painted wall, with different sized apertures. The push-open system used throughout avoids the traditionally omnipresent knobs. From one of these apertures, a non-door lees to one of the upstairs bathrooms, where the white epoxy resin walls set off the glass and steel wash basin. To the left of the stairs, another white painted wall also conceals more cupboard space; one of the openings leads to the elegant main bathroom, divided in three parts with refined but bold wall coverings that separate the areas: in the shower, travertine marble shows off the chromed taps and white sanitary equipment, corium frames the center and the wash basin area, and mirrors surround the dressing area.

The main bedroom is equipped with a large steel based bed, in front of which is a wardrobe completely faced with mirrors. In it is a liquid crystal TV set of which only the screen can be seen; the bed head wall is upholstered in a soft semitransparent curtain material, white and creased, to match the bed cover.

The rooms for the children are amusingly ironic, both functional and refined; no detail has been overlooked. The walls of Niccolò's room are decorated in a zebra pattern of epoxy resin, and the central theme is the stainless steel bed, and the white painted desk. Camilla's room has a bright floor of pale green resin that contains silver CD's.

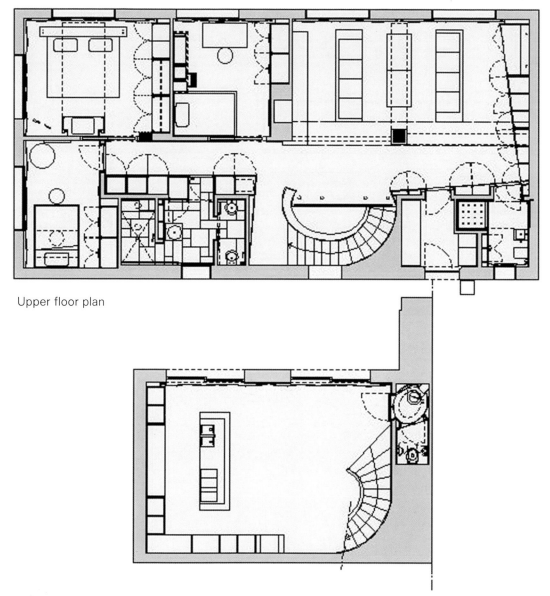

Upper floor plan

Lower floor plan

Defining the little bathroom is its ellipse shaped first area, which contains the cylindrical corium basin, and a second area in which the wall covering suggests blue bubbles underwater. The water closet is surrounded by two semispherical pieces of furniture enameled in white.

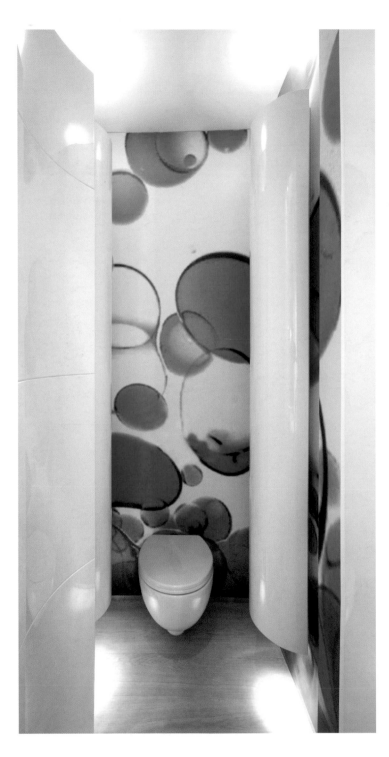

Jay Kammen, KAMMEN

Pablo Loft

Photographs: Massimiliano Bolzonella

San Francisco, USA

In early 2004, Pablo Designs was growing at a rapid rate. They were outgrowing their original design and production studio. The company then acquired a beautiful bright 13,000 square foot simple industrial shell building that originally housed a steel plant. The owner of the company, Pablo Pardo, the renowned lighting designer and entrepreneur was also outgrowing his own San Francisco apartment. Pablo saw the opportunity to create his home under the 40 foot high ceiling of this new building. He consulted architect/designer jay kammen, who had extensive experience transforming many of San Francisco's industrial buildings for new uses, to help create a building within a building. Together they sculpted space and light to create a new structure within the vast volume of the steel plant. The configuration of this installation is based on concentric, interpenetrating volumes; a series of progressively larger volumes inside one another (like a set of russian dolls) all of which nest inside the shell of the existing industrial building. Suspended over the design and production studio, this series of spaces is brought to life by the dynamic transmission of light. Daylight passes from the larger elements to the smaller ones: it enters from the large existing industrial windows, is modulated by the walls (of different heights) and filters through strategic openings into the walls. Artificial light moves in the opposite direction, both directly and indirectly, from the smallest volumes to the larger ones and is modulated by flexible light fixtures (designed by pablo) that can be adjusted to suit the hour and the mood. the materials and finishes are simple and clean in order to act merely as frames or as lenses for the play of light, space and the life that happens within them. The new loft space space functions perfectly as a home for Pablo and as a space to entertain and impress customers of Pablo Designs.

Floor plan

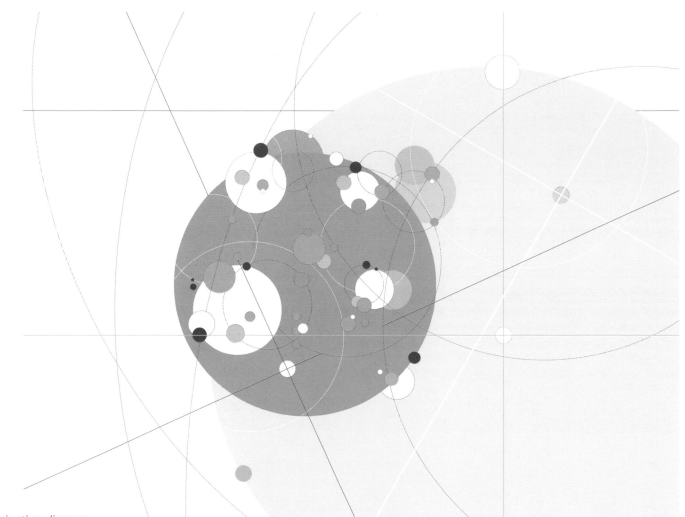

Illumination diagram

Section

DATE DUE